Introduction

For the last 50 years I have been fortunate to work as a PGA professional, training, studying and enjoying everything that this great game can offer. From 1989 to 2004 I was the national coach to the Golfing Union of Ireland (GUI) and it was a privilege to work with so many talented young players who achieved great success both, as individuals and team players.

I would like to offer my sincere thanks to the GUI, their officials and players for having confidence in my work and giving me the opportunity of working with such a talented group of athletes.

When players and teams are successful in any sport everyone wants to know the reason or the secret of their success, such questions have been asked of me many times. What method do you teach? What systems did you use to help players develop and to reach their potential? These are good questions and there is no simple answer. I was working with individuals of different age groups, with their own unique mixture of strengths, weaknesses, personalities and physical capabilities. Humans are not perfect and there are many challenges which need to be addressed.

The following pages reveal my overall philosophy along with some of my many experiences and several specific ideas which I have applied during my career. I trust that you will find some useful information which may help you to improve and enjoy this wonderful game.

Acknowledgements

I would like to thank John Bird for preparing the three different formats, creating the website and organising the online publishing. I would also like to thank my son, Tony Bennett, and his wife, Sue, for making some adjustments to the original text and the initial proofreading. Thank you also to Keith Hick for the final proofreading and a special thank you also to my wife, Sylvia, for all her support.

After completing the text of this book, Rory McIIroy went on to win the US Open and Darren Clarke became the Champion Golfer at The Open in Sandwich. They joined fellow Countrymen Padraig Harrington and Greame McDowell as major winners. Between them they have now won a total of six major championships in the space of four years (2007 to 2011). What a remarkable achievement for these players and the Country of Ireland.

All have given thanks for the help, which they received especially in their early careers, to the Golfing Union of Ireland, in arranging competitions, travel, and coaching. The officials, staff and coaches of the Golfing Union of Ireland are to be congratulated on their contribution to Irish golf over the years.

Foreword by Padraig Harrington

"I first met Howard in 1988 as a 16 year old off a handicap of two, when he was the national coach of Ireland. Previous to that I had limited coaching so little did I know that Howard would still be my coach when I turned pro eight years later and for over a decade in total.

What was noticeable about Howard was that he treated everyone as individuals - he taught the player rather than impose a particular style on him and was encouraging of all players. He certainly never gave the impression that he judged players when they played poorly, and as long as the player did his preparation correctly and was giving 100% he was always very supportive.

He worked on the fundamentals and the art of playing the game and despite a holistic approach he emphasised the importance of the short game and the mental side. He encouraged us to be competitive, teaching us some wonderful short game practice drills, many of which I still use and, in fact, Howard is the only short game coach I've ever had.

Certain traits that he emphasised - strong mental game, good work ethic, determination, discipline - can be seen in my game today, as they were instilled in me in my formative years and will never be forgotten.

He was open minded and encouraged us to go further into our games by reading books on the mental side, which led to my introduction to Bob Rotella. He was very generous in sharing his knowledge, which is the essence of this book.

Howard loves the game of golf and is not interested in what the game can do for him. The etiquette and rules of the game are very important to him and this is borne out in his coaching style.

Howard is a mild mannered man and only rarely does he "lose the head" – the only time I witnessed it was when a certain good player had no interest in being at a coaching session and was therefore wasting the time of the group, much to Howard's displeasure!

I usually saw Howard in Ireland and often went to see him in Southport, when I would stay at his house, which is where I got to know his wife Sylvia and his family, who were always very welcoming.

I have much to thank Howard for in the development of my career and all readers of this book must also thank him for sharing his golf knowledge, whilst benefitting a very worthy cause."

Padraig Harrington - November 2011

Some words from Lora Fairclough

"Inspirational, calming, enthusiastic and motivational are a few key words that come to mind when I reflect on the hours spent on practice grounds and telephone conversations with Howard Bennett.

Having kept all my notes that both Howard and I made as a 14 year old and upwards, these are the ones that I have continued to use during 21 years on tour. His wisdom has never left my golfing mind and I can hear myself speaking sometimes as Howard spoke to me, all those years ago.

Howard's teaching manner and principals were always so relaxing, there was humour thrown in when needed and required, compassion when the golfing gods weren't quite on your side and more importantly, the goodness that runs through this man's veins, should be bottled and sold!! A kinder, gentler soul you couldn't wish to meet and I for one have been very grateful and blessed for both his and his wife Sylvia's knowledge and friendship."

Lora Fairclough - November 2011

Critique

Relatively few books written about golf deserve the status of a 'must read' for students of the game. Stories – Observation – Suggestions falls into this category for all who aspire to optimise their potential and applies to the club golfer as equally as it does to those at the pinnacle of the game.

The book has universal appeal and articulates golf's most fundamental secret: control of the mind, and lives up to its title. Howard lays bare his beliefs, honed over several decades, in his own words and without the aid of a ghost writer.

Over complication and over coaching are two of the greatest retarders in understanding the purity and simplicity of golf. Howard Bennett enables the reader to understand the importance of the KISS (Keep It Simple Stupid) acronym with several others of his own and those coined by accomplished sportsmen and women.

A balance is effectively struck between genders to encourage men and women to understand and appreciate the relative strengths and weaknesses associated with their respective golf game.

The book draws upon golf related wisdom gleaned from a variety of sources, intermingled with Howard's lifetime experiences in coaching and encouraging golfers, many of whom were at the outset of their career. As such, the book deserves its place as a 'golfer's companion', to be retained as a constant reminder of the power of the mind to shape one's life in golf.

Keith Hick, FISTC MSAI AIAM - January 2012.

Stories

The GUI
Padraig Harrington - The first meeting

After being appointed national coach to the GUI one of my first assignments was to take a coaching weekend for 16 boys and youths from the national panel which was to be held at Woodbrook Golf Club, Bray, County Dublin. Checking through the list of names and handicaps of those who were to attend, the only name I recognised was a young man called Leslie Walker who had won the British Boys Amateur Championship in 1986 at Seaton Carew. After introducing myself to the panel and explaining the format, I started to film them as they hit a range of full shots. This gave me the opportunity to open a dialogue with each player, ask a few questions and retain a copy of the golf swing that they had brought to the session. As the training progressed I analysed each swing and explained my assessment to each of the players before setting each a personalised programme.

During that first weekend session I met Padraig Harrington for the first time. He was a young man, 16 years of age with a handicap of two. Padraig had a good attitude and asked many questions. It didn't take me long to notice that he had a great 'desire' (Padraig described this as a 'want') to improve and was prepared to pay the price in both time and effort. Padraig gave an honest assessment of the level of golf he was playing at that time and revealed that he felt there were parts of his game that he needed to improve. He believed that there was always something to be learnt from observing other golfers of various handicaps and from different situations which occurred during a round of golf. Padraig took me a little by surprise when stating, "as iron sharpens iron: so one man sharpens another". This struck me as unusual from a young man of sixteen. Another indication of his thinking and positive attitude was when we were filming his swing, I said, "not many good golfers like missing their shots to the left," his immediate reply was, "I don't either."

As I had limited time to work with the players, it was very important to prepare a schedule for each training session that ensured enough quality time to meet the player's needs. I was aware that I would be the only qualified PGA (Professional Golfers' Association) coach present at the training with 16 players. This in itself was a challenge. I had inherited a coaching programme which had previously suited the needs of the time and the coach rather than the needs of the players. For the first training I went along with what was in place, but promised myself that changes would have to be made to enable us to achieve success at boys, youths and senior levels.

A big advantage that I enjoyed as national coach of the GUI was being able to work with all the panels. It gave me continuity and allowed me to see the players progress from one age group to the

Damian McGraine & Leslie Walker

next; it really became like a large family.

Damien McGraine has shown that if you have the desire, apply discipline, hard work, and perseverance then it is possible to succeed. Damien won the Irish Boys in 1987 and at 20 years of age became the assistant professional to Joey Purcell, the PGA professional at Portmarnock Golf Club. He played on the Irish PGA circuit, MasterCard Tour, Challenge Tour and then went to the European Tour School on five occasions. Damien was club professional at Wexford Golf Club while competing on the European Tour and tasted success with his maiden tour win in the Volvo China Open in Shanghai during 2008. Damien deserves his success and I feel certain there are more to come.

Laying good foundations

Applying the basic fundamentals to most things in life is important and golf is no different, especially when working with youngsters. Preparing good foundations is the most important element and a precursor to a player's progression and any eventual success that they may enjoy. These are the building blocks which must be in place to help them throughout their careers.

The first film that I took of Padraig's swing was when he was 16 years of age and it confirmed that improvements were necessary to both his grip and posture. These adjustments would enable him to have a good foundation from which to build. Most improvements start with the position at address.

During the ten years that I had the privilege of working with Padraig, he always wanted to have a part of his game to work on; it might have been his technique, short game, fitness or the mental game. I had introduced and encouraged Padraig and all the national panel to read the books and listen to the works of sports psychologist Bob Rotella, author of, 'Golf is not a game of perfect', 'The golf of your dreams' and many other easy to read books on the mind game. Not surprisingly, over the last few years Padraig has worked personally with Bob Rotella with great success.

When laying good foundations I believe the biggest influence for a youngster is the guidance and support from their family, it plays such an important role in their development and will stay with them throughout their lives. We only need to look at Tiger Woods, Lewis Hamilton, the Williams sisters and others to recognise this. Padraig's father Paddy, and mother Breda, gave great support to him and his brothers.

The years 1990 - 1998

At the end of each competition season, which in the amateur game was by the first week of October, Padraig would usually ask "what do I need to work on during the winter?" He wanted to make sure that he was constantly working towards improvement and did not waste any time. He always needed to feel prepared for the next season.

1990 Historic Triple Crown wins by Ireland's team, Conway, North Wales

Back row: H Bennett, P McGinley, K Kearney, G McNeill, G Golden (President), P Harrington, D Errity, N Goulding, J Fanagan

Front row: L McNamara, N Anderson, G Crosby (Captain), G McGimpsey, M Gannon

In 1990 Padraig made his first full International debut alongside his good friend Jody Fanagan. They had formed a strong foursome partnership when representing Leinster in the Irish interprovincial matches and it continued into both their International and Walker Cup careers where they became a formidable partnership. In 1990 the Irish team won both the Home Internationals and the Triple Crown in Conway with Padraig winning all six of his matches.

The overall result was decided on the last putt of the final match on the 18th green, when Liam McNamara had the pressure of sinking the winning putt. The Irish supporters went around the green singing "olé, olé, olé, olé", it was a great moment for Ireland and as always Padraig's parents were there giving their full support.

1990 Victorious Irish officials & supporters

Back Row: F Perry, G Crosby (Captain), G Golden (President), J Greene,
H Bennett, L McNamara, N Goulding, P Foley

Kneeling: M Gannon, D Errity, J Fanagan, P Harrington, K Kearney,
G McNeill, P McGinley, Paddy Harrington

1991 Home International winners, County Sligo, Rosses Point, Ireland.

Back row: R Hutton, R Burns, J Fanagan, T Corridan, L McNamara,
R Coghlan, H Bennett, D O'Sullivan.

Seated: N Golding, G McNeill, D Reidy (President), R Staunton (Captain),
G McGimpsey, P Harrington

The 1991 team had five changes from the previous year; all the matches were very close, the passionate home support helped in winning the Internationals for the second year running. As recognition for the win County Sligo Golf Club gave honorary membership to all the players. It was a great honour.

Padraig was picked to play in the 1991 Walker Cup match played at Portmarnock Golf Club in Ireland. It came as a nice surprise for him as the selectors had decided he would be an asset to the team both as an individual player and as a foursome's partner to Paul McGinley. The result did not go Great Britain and Ireland's way with the USA winning by 14 points to 10.

The 1991 Walker Cup was a great learning experience for Padraig but he was disappointed in his own performance, he felt that he had learnt a great deal but would need to gain more distance from the tee. During Padraig's amateur career he saw his standard shot as a straight to fade ball flight, which gave him great control and consistency but he sacrificed some distance. I

Padraig after being selected for his first Walker Cup.

assured him that as he worked on his fitness and improved his swing technique that his distance would improve, but to obtain maximum distance he would need to change to a straight to draw ball flight, Padraig however was not keen to make the change. As a coach, I believe that it is important for the player to take responsibility to think for themselves and it is from these decisions that the player will stand or fall. Padraig was good at making decisions, determined when setting his personal goals and able to concentrate on the process of achieving them rather than focussing on the results.

The 1992 Home Internationals were held at Prestwick Golf Club, Scotland. History was made by the Irish International Team when they completed a feat that had never before been achieved in their 70 years history, that of winning the Home Internationals three years running 1990/91/92.

1992 Home International winners

Back row: R Burns, G Murphy, P Harrington, T Corridan, K Kearney, J Fanagan, H Bennett

Seated: A Morrow, L McNamara, L Reidy (President) R Staunton (Captain), G McGimpsey, N Goulding, K Nolan

"To Prestwick belongs the momentous claim of being the cradle of Championship Golf, the club launched the Open and staged it on twenty-four occasions and for historical correctness the first

Open took place on Wednesday 17th October 1860". *"THE OPEN, Golf's Oldest Major", published by Rizzoli International*

In 1992 Padraig was selected for the Great Britain & Ireland team to play against the Rest of Europe. Padraig's inclusion in the team confirmed his steady progress and meant that the selectors had him in mind for the next Walker Cup to be played in America at Interlachen. The result of the 1993, Walker Cup was a convincing win for the USA by 15 points to 5. Looking back on his two Walker Cup appearances in 1991 and 1993 Padraig felt that he had gained a considerable amount of knowledge but admitted he was a little inexperienced at the time. Once again he felt more distance was needed with his tee shots, to which I gave the same reply that I had given him after the 1991 match, but again he was not keen to make the change, although the seed had been firmly planted.

Padraig turned 21 years of age in 1994 and promptly went on to win the West of Ireland Championship (one of Ireland's major amateur events) on the County Sligo Links Course at Rosses Point. I believe that this win gave him tremendous

Jody and Padraig

confidence for the 1995 season in which he won two of Ireland's major amateur championships, the Irish Open and the Irish Close and finished runner-up in both the South of Ireland and the North of Ireland Championships.

The 1995 Walker Cup match was to be played at Royal Porthcawl Golf Club in Wales and for the third time Padraig was selected. After two consecutive defeats the 14 points to 10 win for GB&I was met with great celebration. Padraig played and won two foursomes matches with his great friend Jody Fanagan. One of these matches was played against Tiger Woods & J Harris, which the Irish players won 2&1. Who at that time would have predicted that Padraig and Tiger would meet head to head in future play offs? Jody was undefeated in his three matches and Padraig had secured three from a possible four points. This was Padraig's most successful year as an amateur and his decision to turn professional after the Walker Cup was no surprise.

Padraig's priority was now to obtain his European Tour card. He was reasonably confident and felt that if he could get through the first stage of qualifying (36 holes), then he would have a good chance in the final stage which was to be played over six rounds. As the history books will tell he passed both tests and duly obtained his European Tour playing privileges.

At that time all players who earned their cards were invited to a training and education week focussed on helping them to understand what was required when joining the European Tour. The 'Apollo' week was traditionally held in Spain during the month of January.

On his return home to Ireland from that week I received a phone call asking if it was convenient for him to come over to England and discuss certain points which had come up during 'Apollo' week. We met during the last week of January (1996) at Newark Golf Club where my son Tony was the club PGA professional and where I coached when not busy with the GUI. Padraig's first question for me concerned a point raised by the two golf swing coaches and it was related to the old question which we had faced before: whether or not he should continue with his stock shot of straight to fade or change it to straight to draw?

Padraig and Tony Bennett, at Newark Golf Club

After we discussed the question and analysed the issues around a possible change, he asked me directly, "what do you think?"

Knowing that this could be a major influence on his future career, I reminded Padraig of our conversations after the two Walker Cup matches in 1991 & 1993 where my advice had been that his stock shot should be straight to draw which would give him the necessary distance he needed for the tee shots and would be more suited to links golf. As always I reminded him that the decision had to be his and without any hesitation his reply was, "we will do it". This showed great mental strength and revealed how much he wanted to progress to the next level. He was prepared to make the necessary changes and sacrifices to move forward.

Working with Padraig on the practice ground

Padraig's next goal was to retain his tour card for the following year and he set about achieving it by playing in the first eight tournaments and successfully making every cut. Without any break his ninth event was the Spanish Open where he not only made the cut but he went on to win the tournament, so earning him a two year exemption on tour and a place in The Open. Quite an achievement for a rookie less than three months into his professional career.

During the early tournaments Padraig and I tried to meet every three to four weeks for a couple of days to exchange ideas and see how things were developing. During a session at Aroeira Golf Club in Portugal we discussed his putting grip; specifically whether he should use his normal right hand below left grip or left hand below right. He felt confident with either of the two grips and this was to a large extent determined by the line and pace of the putt. I asked him which grip he eventually wished to adopt? "Left below right was his reply" and I suggested that he use the grip he felt most comfortable with during the changeover period. At the time some TV commentators and journalists thought Padraig might have a challenging time as a professional if at this early stage in his career he was unsure about his putting grip, (even though he was holing most of his putts). By the end of his first year on tour his putting grip was left below right, the rest is history.

The 1996 Open at Royal Lytham was Padraig's first Open. After a couple of practice rounds we were waiting for the draw sheet to be posted to check starting times and to see who he would be drawn with for the first two days. His caddy, John O'Reilly, liked having a joke or two and said I hope we don't get two big names. Fred Couples and Mark McCumber came out of the draw, (they were both in the top 10 in the world at the time), Padraig really looked forward to competing in the Open and playing with two of the world's best golfers. In the first two rounds he scored 68-68 which kept him in touch with the leaders, a 3rd round score of 73 and a final round of 71 helped him to 18th position and a very satisfactory first Open.

After representing Ireland in the 1996 Dunhill Cup at St Andrews, Padraig was ready for a well-earned rest; he had achieved and surpassed the goals he had set for himself.

The 1997 Open at Royal Troon showed more progress for Padraig, with scores of 75-69-69-67 to finish 5th. He also won the World Cup of Golf at Kiawh Island with Paul McGinley and again represented Ireland at the Dunhill Cup at St Andrews. Padraig was a little down at not making the Ryder Cup team which was played at Valderama in Spain. The captain, Seve Ballesteros, had to select the one remaining place in the team, it was a choice between José Maria Olazabal or Padraig. Seve decided on José Maria.

The first US Open which Padraig played was in 1998 held at the Olympic Club, San Francisco and all the competitors agreed it was a very stern test. The winner was US Open specialist Lee

Janzen with a four round total of 280 which was level par, Padraig had rounds of 73-72-76-72 to finish in 32nd place.

Johnny always wanted a chat on the practice ground. With Tiger Woods & John Daly

There were many positives for Padraig from the 1998 US Open, especially his course management, overall short game and mental

With the Irish supporters, US Open 1998

approach, but he was disappointed and felt he lacked the necessary technique to compete successfully at that level of the game. Serious thought was given by both of us as to what was needed to be done and it was agreed to meet up again at the 1998 Open at Royal Birkdale. I believed he would do

well at Royal Birkdale as he liked links golf, also his previous two Open finishes suggested another good performance was possible.

At the beginning of the week we met on the practice ground and I could see from Padraig's body language that he wasn't himself. After our initial greetings we discussed the details for the week. He had been considering what should be done with regards to his swing technique, he felt another opinion was needed and had asked Bob Torrance, I had always respected Padraig's honesty and decisions he made during the ten years of working together and this occasion was no different. Bob was a good choice of coach and time has proven this to be the case. That week was an emotional week for both of us, as unfortunately Padraig missed the cut but he made up for it ten years later by winning in style and earning his second Open Championship.

I have many good memories of our years working together and to see him develop over the last few years as a person, golfer, role model and ambassador for the game of golf has been an immense pleasure.

I am sure he has given great pleasure and pride to his family and to those who have supported him throughout his career, no doubt there is more to come. For me it has been a privilege over the years to have had the opportunity of working with Padraig and all the players of the GUI.

Thank you all.

With Bob Torrance on the practice ground where he is very happy to be with his pupils

Darren Clarke (King Prawn)

Before the start of every competition season the GUI held a training week for the senior squad, usually in the last week of March. In 1990 it was held at Penina in the Algarve and for the players, officials and coach it was a busy six days which included daily 18 hole match play contests in the morning and 18 holes of stroke play every afternoon. We still had to find time to fit in technical work, special practice routines and individual sessions with each player. The panel consisted of many fine players, those who had proven themselves at Full International Level and some very exciting young prospects.

The four round stroke play event was won by Darren Clarke who during his 4th round had four birdies at the par 3 holes and finished with an excellent round of 66, played from the very back tees, but that was not his only accomplishment of the week. When we arrived at Penina the mealtime arrangements had been arranged by the GUI officials. The hotel management felt it would be a good idea to have a buffet for the evening meal so that it would save time whilst allowing everyone to choose what they liked to eat. The buffet on the first night was magnificent, especially the king prawns and Darren took a real liking to them.

With Darren, (King Prawn) 1990

The players enjoyed the food so much that the table was completely empty by the time we had finished. The management quickly realised that the budget did not cover the cost, so needless to say on the remaining nights we were presented with a set menu, but by then Darren had acquired the nickname 'King Prawn'.

In 1990 Darren decided to turn professional. It was a surprise to many because he was certain to be picked for the next Walker Cup match, but he believed that his next step was to play professional golf on the PGA European Tour and felt there was no point in waiting any longer. On the golf course his athletic build gave him a certain aura; he was an exciting player, hit the ball a tremendous distance and owned a handicap of +5.

Training week at Penina 1990

Back row standing: R Burns, F McCarroll (GUI), Dr Jnr Morris, F Howley, D Clarke, E Powe
S Keenan, K Kearney, R Staunton(GUI), J Fanagan, M Craddock(GUI).

Kneeling: P Hogan, M Gannon, Howard Bennett, P Harrington, P Gribben,
L McNamara, G Crosby (Capt), A Pierse, N Golding.

GUI 'Champion's Dinner'

Padraig and his wife, Caroline, invited my wife Sylvia and I to the first GUI champion's dinner on January 7th, 2008 at Carton House Dublin, to celebrate all the Irish winners of both amateur and professional tournaments throughout the 2007 season. The highlights, of course were Padraig's win at Carnoustie and Rory McIlroy winning the silver medal at the same Open.

With Padraig at the champion's dinner

With Rory McIlroy and John Caldwell
at the champion's dinner

Do your dreams come true?

During my career I have dreamt of achieving many things, some have come to fruition, others until now have not (mainly because of my lack of commitment). One dream that did come true was working as national coach to the GUI. The GUI was the first golf union or federation to be founded, formed on 12th October 1891 in Portrush, County Antrim, and they have been at the forefront of progress in the amateur game ever since.

It was during my first coaching session with the national panel that I realised something had to change to address the complete coaching needs of the players and empower the coaches in their work. This I felt would ensure that the GUI kept moving towards the realisation of their objectives.

Looking at the talent and flair of Irish golfers over the years and what they have achieved both in amateur and professional golf is quite remarkable. I was aware that Irish senior teams and individuals were winning at international level and yet was surprised that the boys and youths were not. Talented players with flair were in abundance but the results were not coming. It was my opinion that the coaching and support had to improve to enable us to achieve success at both the boys and youths level and by doing so the senior team would also benefit as the younger players pushed for senior honours.

My short term goals / dreams for the national panels were to separate the boys and youths panels. They consisted of 16 players in each and would come together during four weekends over the winter months at a golf complex in the Dublin area. We would also have present at the coaching sessions the PGA qualified coaches from the four provinces, along with specialists in fitness, diet, rules and the mind game.

The long term dream was for the GUI to have their headquarters and training centre at a venue close to Dublin.

European Youth Team Champions 1994
Standing: Peter Lawrie, Andrew McCormack, Eamon Brady,
Stephen Maloney and the Finland representative.

Seated: Keith Nolan, Jimmy Greene (manager)
Michael McGinley (Captain) and Ritchie Coughlin

Before the competition season started in April, there would be a coaching week in the warm climates of Spain or Portugal. These sessions would have eight boys and eight youths with the main focus being on sharpening up their short game, heightening their competitive edge and some critical team building exercises.

Worthy dreams and goals take time to achieve as we all know.

Only with assistance and help from colleagues and relevant organisations can we hope to achieve and certainly in my case it was the officials of the GUI who have various committees that were very supportive.

In my role as national coach I was responsible to the convenor of the training committee, a gentleman by the name of Jimmy Greene, who was a great supporter of the GUI as most of the unpaid officials were. On our first meeting Jimmy asked me in which areas could we improve, both in the short term and the long term "How long have you got?" I said. His reply was "take as long as you like I am a good listener". Jimmy was true to his word and took the suggestions back to the relevant committees for their approval. Over the next few months and years improvements gradually started to be implemented and it is well documented now that the GUI moved into their new offices and have their coaching facilities and complex centralised at the prestigious Carton House Hotel near Dublin.

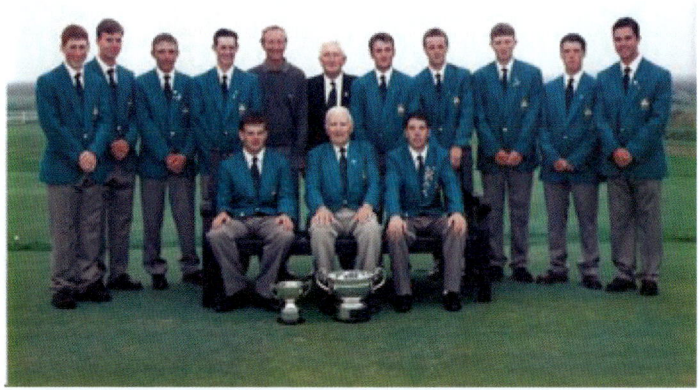

Winners Boys Home International 1997 at Royal North Devon

Back row: M Sullivan, M McDermott, C Moriarty, D Carroll, H Bennett, C Gannon, G McDowell, M Hoey, R Symes, G Wardlow, M Campbell
Seated: D Jones, J Greene (Captain) and L Dalton.

Graeme McDowell was US Open Winner 2010
Michael Hoey was British Amateur Champion 2001
All of the young men in the team have won major titles in Ireland

In these pictures you may be able to identify some of the young men who came through the GUI coaching programme that have

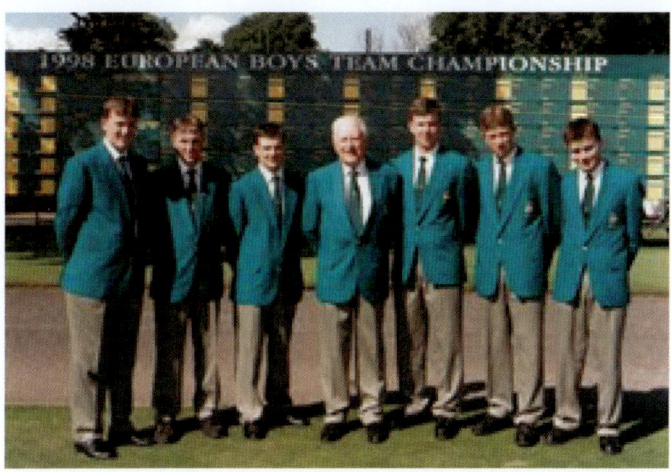

Boys European Champions 1998 at Gullane Golf Club Scotland

Mervin Owen, Shaun McTernan, David Jones, Jimmy Greene (Captain)
Michael McDermott, Robin Symmns and Justin Kehoe

gone on to achieve golfing success.

In the year 2000 the GUI continued with their forward planning of the national coaching sessions and introduced an under 15 boys panel in order to catch players at an earlier age, so giving them the opportunity to benefit from national coaching.

Rory McIlroy came into the panel in 2002 and his personal coach Michael Bannon, who was the Ulster provincial coach, was also present at the sessions. Although only 13 years of age Rory's presence added interest which helped the panellists as he already had a handicap of 3. There was always a lot of leg pulling and friendly rivalry which helped us with team building and even though Rory was the youngest, (and the smallest) he gave as much as he got and his golf soon earned him the respect of the other panellists, GUI officials and all the coaching staff. It was only a few years later that he earned worldwide respect for his game. It is quite remarkable and much credit must go to his parents and his coach Michael Bannon for giving him such sound advice. Of course Rory has worked hard at the game he obviously loves and the main credit therefore must go to him.

Coaches working with young boys and girls in various sports are often asked which youngster is going to be a star of the future. What a question. Most of the time you have an idea who will continue to improve, but to forecast which player is going to be a major winner in golf is almost impossible.

During my 15 years working with the GUI, I was privileged to work with so many talented young men, major championship winners: Padraig Harrington (The Open Champion 2007, 2008 and US PGA Champion 2008) and Graeme McDowell (US Open Champion 2010), Ryder Cup players Paul McGinley, Rory McIlroy (US Open Champion 2011), British Amateur Champions Michael Hoey (2001) and Brian McElhinney (2005) along with many others who have won prestigious tournaments at amateur and professional levels. Who knows how many more will add a Major to their C.V? Time will tell.

It is interesting to know what the winners of Major Championships believe contributed to their success. Tom Watson who won two Masters 1977 & 1981, one US Open 1982, and The Open on five occasions 1975, 1977, 1980, 1982 & 1983, makes the following points which obviously must still ring true and continue to work well for Tom as in 2010 he won both the British & US Senior Opens.

According to Tom Watson

- I needed a little magic, a little luck and all the skill I could muster and the best thinking I was capable of.
- No matter how well you hit the ball, you have to think well to start with, have to be aware of your options and pick the right one.
- I won the tournament as much with my mind as with my clubs.
- You have to think out every shot, you have to do that anywhere.
- I told my caddie, Bruce Edwards, just to keep reminding me to keep my tempo smooth.
- I always play in a vacuum, I say very little and at times I'm barely aware of what is happening to my playing partner or anything else.
- It was a missed opportunity, but there was nothing to do but put it out of my mind.
- My adrenalin was flowing and I was extremely intense.
- The pressure was gone; I had control of the situation.
- I'd had a little magic in me and I was the Open Champion.
- I am basically an aggressive player, but I'll play safely when the potential penalty is too great and I'm in a position to win a tournament. I'll also play safely or more aggressively depending on how I feel that particular day.
- Remember that not even the best players in the world hit all the greens in regulation.

The Working Together Model at the Heart of Irish Phenomenon

This article by Dennis Shaw was included in the PGA magazine Aug-2011

Although nobody could have realised the enormous significance of it at the time, the 15 years beginning in 1988 was a period in Irish golf history when the seeds of the golden harvest of talent, currently being reaped, were carefully and lovingly sown.

During those years, the capacity of the PGA of Ireland (PGAI) to provide the professional coaching expertise for fine-tuning the extraordinary raw amateur talent unearthed by the Golfing Union of Ireland (GUI), created a Working Together model that lies at the very heart of the PGAs of Europe's philosophy.

"There is no question that the cash and resources provided by the GUI in enabling their best amateurs to progress in the leading tournaments, and the coterie of PGA professionals around Ireland coaching them up to elite level, is at the basis of the recent success that we have enjoyed," said Michael McCumisky, PGAI secretary.

"The groundwork was put down by Howard Bennett (PGA Master Professional, pictured) when he was our national coach and now it is being continued by Neil Manchip (also a PGA professional)."

As a result, a combination of inspired education, boundless effort and enthusiasm, attention to the minutest detail and fortunate timing, has spawned the growth of what the world currently recognises as the Irish Golf Phenomenon and prompts the question: "How does this little island manage to win so much?"

Quite a haul, indeed: in some four years a quartet of Irish players in Padraig Harrington, Graeme McDowell, Rory McIlroy  and Darren Clarke have won SIX Major championships. Between them, also, they have won barrow loads of global tournaments and riches. Add the name of Paul McGinley and you also have a quintet of Ryder Cup winners. Astonishing...!

In underlining how professional coaching can harness any array of basic skills, temperaments and attitudes, PGAI secretary McCumisky pointed out the wide differences between Ireland's major winners and how those differences have been nurtured towards a similar outcome.

"Harrington was always an outstanding amateur but he wasn't always a winner," Michael recalled. "He's needed to work very hard at it and especially to become keen on the psychology side. Clarke was a more natural player and always had the ability to win things, and in some ways was a ready-made professional while McIlroy, of course, was weaned on golf from the earliest age."

It was back to May 2003 the first public clue to what had been going on just across the Irish Sea from mainland Britain. The GUI threw a farewell party for their retiring National Golf Coach, Howard Bennett who, by then a sexagenarian, was moving back to his native England after a decade and a half of nurturing the best young amateur players that the Emerald Isles could muster.

At that function, described as being 'an emotional one', Howard was handing over the national coaching structure that he had personally fostered and enhanced to be based for the way forward at a thoroughly-modern academy at Carton House along with a successor yet to be selected. The structure that he had painstakingly created was to be continued in a thoroughly modern manner.

One speaker, Harrington, summed up Bennett's impact on both himself and other young players at that time by saying: "I owe Howard Bennett everything. Not a day goes by that I don't play a round or hit a shot and not be reminded of him.

"He has played a big part in what I have done as a player. He'll never know how much I owe him- nor will Paul McGinley or any of the other guys he coached. He often said that practice makes permanent and that is just one of many things I have taken with me. As a coach he worked harder than anyone else in the squad, as hard as any of us who played. He wanted to improve as a coach just as much as we did as players.

"He got us to look at sports psychology and to understand the importance of physical fitness. He helped you to mould your character and the way you lived your life. Howard always spoke  about the Three Ds of discipline, dedication and desire. As he retires he can be proud of the fact that he has been able to contribute to the betterment of the game. He wanted to get better as much as I wanted to get better. His enthusiasm was what made him such a great teacher."

As Howard Bennett's son, Tony, the PGAs of Europe's Director of Education, a PGA Master Professional like his father, sums up a triangular scenario of an outstanding young player's career progress: "The federations find the best young players, invite PGA pros to coach them, and then pass them on, gift-wrapped if you like, to the European Tour."

Or as Leif Ohlsson, the recently-retired leading sports educationalist and chairman of the PGAs of Europe Education Committee would put it: "Only when the most talented players are taught by the best coaches is excellence achieved in sport."

This can, of course, be a fairly routine process, but in this particular period, it was no such thing. Just appearing over the horizon to join the national squad - all boyish charm, curly hair and outrageous talent – was Rory McIlroy.

Howard's appointment made him responsible for three squads of sixteen players, namely Boys, Youths and Seniors. They were assembled from four provinces, Ulster, Munster, Leinster and Connacht. One of the regular parts of the programme, for instance, was training weeks abroad which, he discovered, involved them playing 36 holes of golf each day.

This he changed to just 18 holes daily so that the other half day could be taken up by a range of subjects including fitness, physiotherapy, diet, psychology and knowledge of the rules. This led to the provincial coaches being invited to join in, share knowledge and ideas. "We began to sing from the same hymn sheet." he recalled. "We wanted to ensure that every subject was covered.

"We were very fortunate to have players like Padraig, Darren, Graeme and Paul in these squads and then there was another stroke of good fortune when an under-15 squad was formed with Rory McIlroy in it." he added. "Also, one of the provincial coaches was Michael Bannon, Rory's coach."

Eventually this fine tuning of a basic structure that was already there meant that Howard was able to build what amounted to one large national golf squad, across the age groups, all working to a similar pattern, all knowing each other and helping each other. Had it been officially named GolfTeam Ireland it would not have been a misnomer.

Bennett senior readily concedes that one important way in which benefits were enjoyed was that while Ireland has its well-known political and religious divides, Irish golf does not. It is one golfing nation. It has one set of golfing principles, one golfing public that breathes its enthusiasm and energy into all of its players. Golf is its own religion. Its own politics.

Another crucial fact was that, along the way, he decided that the coaching of all of the elite squads needed to be centralised for training purposes under himself and the four national coaches, assembled from across all four provinces, something that had never been done before. The GUI settled for a site just outside Dublin in the CityWest Hotel vicinity as a temporary measure though the ultimate aim of the National Golf Academy that was eventually realised with the birth of Carton House.

"It was all common sense and logic really, and a privilege to work with so many talented young men and the GUI. They made it easy to make improvements," he emphasises. "Ireland has lots of sporting talent and the Irish people love their sport so passionately it is hard to put it into words...I thoroughly enjoyed my time there and, to be honest, I miss it. But it's been a thrill to see them do so well. When you think of the size of the place, I doubt if any other country around the world, not even the United States, can compare with their winning six majors with four different players in four years."

If any further proof were needed of the attention to detail that has gone into the preparation of Ireland's elite players for greater things it might well have been there in Darren Clarke's acceptance speech at Royal St George's.

"One feature I felt we had overlooked in providing teaching for the players was the winner's speech," Howard explains. "I raised this at one of our centralised meetings and one of the coaches said that he had once failed to win a tournament that he should have won because he was so nervous going up the 18th at the prospect of having to make a speech. We advised the players on how to go about it and to always have a speech prepared so that they didn't have to worry about it on the last green."

And Darren did rather well, didn't he? It may not have the official title, but GolfTeam Ireland, of which the elite players of all age groups are a part, lives on. And as Michael McCumisky adds as an ominous postscript: "There is going to be an under-13 team, now..."

Ladies golf

Over the years I have worked with some very talented and determined women golfers, both individually and as part of a team. These women have always given their best and applied themselves well to the different forms of practice and preparation which was required and have been extremely serious regarding the application of the rules of golf.

There are slight differences which we have to consider when coaching women, strength and flexibility are the main factors. Generally it has been my experience that women are not as strong as men, but tend to be more flexible. This means that their balance and timing when swinging the club has to be emphasised but once these differences have been taken into consideration the same basic principles can be applied.

Big strides have been made in both professional and top amateur ladies golf. Many women players have not only improved the distance which they hit the ball but have made a significant improvement in their short game, fitness and general preparation, which has contributed to the rise in standards.

It has been said by certain TV commentators that most male members of golf clubs would benefit from watching the top women golfers instead of the top men. There are great lessons to be learned from the way in which women swing the golf club and most men would be capable of incorporating it into their own game. Trying to emulate the way Tiger Woods, Lee Westwood and other top professionals swing the golf club would be difficult for all but the most athletic man. I would certainly go along with this advice.

I have been fortunate to have had the opportunity to coach winners from the Ladies European Tour, top amateur champions in both individual and team championships and competent competitors at both country and club levels.

Just a few of those talented and determined women

Lora Fairclough was one of many young golfers that have had a very supportive family system. Father Gerry, who was himself a very good athlete, helped with her fitness, travel arrangements and performed the role of caddy on many occasions.

Working with Lora

At an early age Lora quickly picked up the basic fundamentals of the golf swing and played mainly by feel. Her home course Chorley Golf Club, 'Hall on the Hill', was generally undulating and I believe that this gave her a good understanding of the different shapes of shots required and a good vision of shots on and around the green. Lora was also allowed to play from the men's tees, from which I feel she gained good experience of scoring and helped her to develop into a fine young player and a real competitor.

I first had the opportunity of working with Lora in 1984. She had a successful amateur career but felt a little disappointed at not making the Curtis Cup team. In January 1991 she turned professional and played on the Ladies European Tour where she had four tournament wins and made the top ten in the order of merit on five occasions between1993 and 1999. Additionally she was also a member of Europe's 1994 Solheim Cup Team.

A skiing accident early in 2010, damaging her cruciate ligament, completely ruled her out of golf for over 12 months. After rehabilitation she started to play golf again with a desire to play a few tournaments during 2011. I know that she will be as determined as ever to try and compete and enjoy the game she loves.

The Irish Ladies Golfing Union (ILGU)

The ILGU invited me to coach their panel of internationals in 1991; the following photograph shows ten of the selected panel

ILGU Ladies Mount Juliet 1991:

Susan O'Gorman, Bridget Gleeson, Lynne Sweeney, Deirdre McMahon, Yvonne Cassidy, Denise McCarthy, Howard Bennett, Eavan Higgins, Mary McKenna, Oonagh Purfield, Ada O'sullivan, Eileen Rose McDaid.

members plus the captain. This was the first weekend session held at the new Mount Juliet Golf Course Kilkenny. They were so enthusiastic and hardworking, in particular Mary McKenna (4th from right), the most experienced and successful in the panel. She constantly took notes and was eager to improve. What a great inspiration to the rest of the panel.

Many of the Ladies went on to win some of Ireland's major amateur tournaments; others have become successful PGA professionals, whilst Ada O'sullivan (2nd from right), apart from winning tournaments, became the captain of the Curtis Cup Team in 2004 at Formby Golf Club, Southport

The Leicester & Rutland Ladies County Team

The Leicester & Rutland County Teams travelled over to Newark Golf Club for coaching from January 1994 until I moved to live in Southport during 1998.

Players & Officials celebrating their two victorys at the 1994 Midland Championship at Cromer Golf Club

Lynn Sleath (Captain), Wendy Greenlees (Vice Captain), Angie Allsop (Midland committee), Jo Morris (winner), Moira Page & Tracy Bourne

When I look back now I really don't know how I ever managed to find the time for this as my itinerary was packed and quite hectic at that time, working with the Golfing Union of Ireland, The Irish Ladies Golf Union, The Royal Air Force teams, plus individual clients. However, I'm very happy that I did manage to help them and I remember they were a very enthusiastic, happy group of golfers making excellent and steady progress during the time that I worked with them.

Most of the lady's had good swings, so we concentrated on the basic fundamentals at address, the importance of a pre shot routine before every shot, the mental game, also the importance of the short game with regards to how successful they would be as a team or individuals.

Sir Henry Cotton

In 1971 during a family holiday at Penina Golf Hotel in the Algarve, I plucked up courage to ask the great man Henry Cotton if I could watch him teach on the practice ground. To say I was apprehensive is putting it mildly, but there was no need to be concerned as his reply was that on every Monday to Saturday he would be on the

Sir Henry Cotton
with Tony & Sylvia Bennett

practice ground from 9.00 until 12.00 and from 15.00 to 18.00.

Every day Mr Cotton played nine holes with an invited 3 ball and said that I was most welcome to attend at any time, what a wonderful opportunity. During the late 1960s and throughout the 1970s, Mr Cotton had talented young players and groups of both professional and amateurs making the journey to Penina for the Maestro's knowledge and advice. Players such as Joe and Roddy Carr, Howard Clark, Mark James, Ken Brown, Nick Faldo and many other PGA professionals, who were seeking to improve their own golf or, like myself, teaching ability.

The time spent with Mr Cotton was always enlightening, interesting and enjoyable, whether it was on the practice ground, playing a round of golf, or during dinner, there was never a dull moment and it was a continual learning experience. Today the PGA would describe it as further education or continuing professional development.

Sir Henry Cotton & Tony Bennett
1974

As Mr Cotton reached his mid-sixties he remained very mentally alert, still looking for new innovations in equipment, technology and coaching. He was continually asking questions and experimenting, always trying to find a better way, not just on golf but on life. No wonder he was a great golfer and a great person. Mr Cotton wrote various books, one in particular entitled "Thanks For The Game" is full of his experiences, his feelings and beliefs on this wonderful game of golf. The information in the book shows that he was well ahead of his time in so many ways. You were never quite sure what was going to happen next when you were in his company.

During one of my visits to Penina an interesting incident took place. Whilst Mr Cotton was having lunch a gentleman politely approached him and asked him if he would be so good as to give a lesson to a young man, who in his opinion was a great prospect and who had a handicap of +4. Mr Cotton asked, "can he play"? Mr Cotton then carried on with his lunch and the gentleman looked a little confused. Thinking that Mr Cotton had not heard what he had said and plucking up courage he once again asked the same question and was given the same reply, "can he play"? By this time the gentleman was really confused and asked, what do you mean sir, "can he play"? Mr Cotton then said, "tell me, what has he won?" This was an important and repeating factor in his assessment of a player and cut to the core of his philosophy.

Together with Penina's three golf professionals
Robin Liddle, José Marcelino, José Lourenco

I often wonder what views Mr Cotton would have had regarding the development of today's golf. The great advances in club and ball technology, golf course architecture, the modern power game and the advancement in golf coaching, I am sure he would have had very interesting observations. Mr Cotton promoted the importance of keeping the game of golf simple and the importance of finding the back of the ball with the club head square. He consistently emphasised that finding the ball (which is the development of a skill which we all have from the day we are born), is vital. "Finding the ball requires only that a player develops a talent he or she already has. Few people have any difficulty in driving a nail squarely into a piece of wood; why then make a complicated thing of hitting a golf ball" (Thanks for the Game 1980).

In order to develop strength and harmony in the hands, wrists and forearms to generate the club head speed required to increase distance and consistency to hit the ball further, Mr Cotton introduced the tyre drill (many current top players are using an impact bag) to complement what they are already working on. "My beliefs and my method have at time been considered antiquated, particularly by power players, but I am happy to let results speak for themselves" (Thanks for the Game 1980). It is not surprising that many of Mr Cotton's drills and key thoughts he himself used during his tournament years, are still being used today by many coaches and players. It was a privilege for my family and I to have spent quality time with Sir Henry Cotton, the friendship and advice will always be with us.

Mr Cotton also championed the cause of young golfers and was a founder member of the Golf Foundation, as you will see from the following article written in the 1970s, he was ahead of his time.

"Strength in the arms is what the youngsters need" (Henry Cotton)

"Just how quickly can a young golfer build himself up from a weak hitter to a powerful striker of the ball? This is a question which interests thousands of youngsters, it is all very well to show a youngster how to swing the club and even give him a classical swing, but if he has no strength in the hands and arms (you can add legs and stomach muscles) to whip the club head through then the best swing in the world availeth him not.

Moving the ball out a decent distance and flying to the green from heavy rough when the occasion occurs is something which does need, without doubt, strength in the arms.

Sir Henry Cotton practicing in 1974

As every teacher knows it is easier to harness power than to make it, and so very few pupils will work hard enough at their practice to give the teacher a chance of fully helping them, many do no sort of golf drill outside their lesson time, this means that progress will be slow, unless by fortune they have adequate golf muscles already.

A good swing is important and I like my pupils to look good when striking the ball, but looks come second to powerful striking even when done my old way, for no one has ever called Arnold Palmer's swing elegant.

Yes I would always settle for Arnold's swing no matter how it is described and some of his knee bending finishes are very special to look at as he weaves all over the place, unleashing his formidable power".

A short poem by Sir Henry Cotton

Sir Henry Cotton created a short poem which he shared with many players

"You cannot play good golf for long unless your hands
and wrists are strong for they alone provide the strength
for great control the extra length which you require to
murder par and hit the golf ball straight and far."

Observations

Inside sport - is professionalism killing sport?

BBC TV screened the above documentary in October 2010.
Following are just some of the questions that were presented to
well-known and very successful sports men and women:

- Can professionalism harm sports men / women as much
  as it helps them?
- Does thinking get in the way of performing?
- Does over coaching stop you doing things by instinct and
  flair?
- Has inspiration been forgotten?
- Has sport become so professional that players are unable
  to have fun?
- Are players being over coached, instead of playing
  instinctively?
- Is too much thinking destroying how to play?

BBC Sports Personality for the years 2009/2010 were Ryan
Giggs and A P McCoy, two names who have been at the top of
their profession for many years. It was fascinating to listen to
their opinions on coaching and its influence on their careers.

A selection of some of the answers / opinions:

- Ryan Giggs (football): I am an instinctive player and play
  like I used to as a kid of 15 years old. The more you get
  coached the less it becomes instinctive. Make the best of
  what you've got and prepare in the right way.

- Mark Ramprakash (cricket): Learn to relax and be expressive, enjoy the limelight.
- A P McCoy (jump jockey): Motivated by the fear of failure, also fear of not being the champion jockey which keeps him going. He feels winning makes it more enjoyable.
- Laura Davies (golfer): Why she keeps going, just loves to win. Find your own formula for practice on what works or what doesn't work for you.
- Usain Bolt (runner): Relax, enjoy the moment and get the job done. Do it with flair and style.
- Roger Federer (tennis): Play fair and enjoy. He loves the distraction of his family and being with them.
- Lewis Hamilton (Formula 1 driver): Feels that he still has the same attitude to driving as when he was racing as a child.
- E.D Smith (cricket): Sport should be competitive and fun.
- Colin Montgomerie (golf): In the Ryder Cup there is no prize money; it is played for the passion of the game. If you enjoy what you do then you will probably do well at it. We all love the Ryder Cup.
- Sir Clive Woodward (rugby coach): The player needs to know what they do, and having that knowledge of what they do will help them to enjoy it and do better.

Some of the findings from the programme

- Sport should be competitive and fun.
- Successful players are no different than when they were a child, the kid is still inside them, they must try to retain that ability.

- To try and think simply and play by instinct.
- Sport used to be about building character, or is it now destroying it?
- General opinions were that most top players managed to remain as a child at heart and played with a childlike freedom.

Players and coaches from various sports who watched the programme Inside Sport would have been interested at some of the answers given by these successful athletes, I certainly found it so. The value and benefits of coaching is one of the many areas of improvements which is discussed when PGA professionals / coaches come together at conventions, seminars and training sessions. The standard of training and further education is of paramount importance to the Professional Golfers Association, which has become a role model for many of sports governing bodies.

Peter Thompson and Laura Davies: natural or feel players?

Peter Thompson and Laura Davies are two great players (from different generations) that reportedly have never had a golf lesson. For many it is amazing to think that they have both managed to achieve so much tournament success.

I believe that we are all given gifts, but relatively few recognise their talents and work hard enough to develop them. There are many people who have been very successful, even though they didn't seem to have all the text book skills and did not conform to a certain model. Many New Orleans jazz musicians, the armed forces sweetheart Dame Vera Lynn and Sir Paul McCartney could not read music. Numerous business and professional people developed without any academic success and sportsmen and women (including golfers) with a wide variety of backgrounds. So how did they succeed, was it by doing things naturally, or by feel?

To be a 'natural' player it takes time, coaching rather than instruction, sound and timely advice, years of dedicated practice. Only then can one become a natural and achieve success.

'Feel' players achieve their success by trial and error and learn more by vision and imitating, (young children are a great example of this). Feel players visualise and feel the golf swing required for a specific shot, they keep it simple, don't get too technical and just focus on playing.

Which category do Peter and Laura fit into? I'll let you decide, but what I do know is that any successful golfer has found out what it is that works for them and that golf primarily is control of self and ball.

Is it easier to succeed in golf today?

Tournament professionals on the various European Tours, amateurs who are selected by their Country for the elite squads at boys, youths and senior levels and those who have been picked to represent their Country at international events, are better prepared and catered for than ever before. Support is available in many areas, technique, psychology, fitness, diet, the availability of practice facilities, equipment, management arrangements and so on, all of which are of great help. I believe it is now more of a challenge for the present and future generations of elite golfers because we are living in a world of instant: coffee, credit, communications and instant gratification. This does not apply to golf or for that matter when learning to be competent in most things in life, such as music, languages, medicine, law and many other highly skilled jobs and professions, it takes time. There are so many more distractions today than 25/30 years ago, individuals wishing to get to the top in any sport today need to be single-minded, have the desire or want to follow their dreams, enjoy the journey and take a long term view to achieving them.

There is an old saying: "You can take a horse to water, but you cannot make it drink". The person that makes it happen (even though they have been given all the help they need) is the player him or herself, they have to take the responsibility for their success or failure.

Attributes of a coach

During my early years as a young professional golfer when learning the different aspects of the profession, (there were many and even more today), I used to ask myself what are the attributes of a good coach. I studied many of the books by well-known teachers /coaches and made every effort to watch some of them teach. At that time John Jacobs had a number of driving ranges throughout the country. A golf professional friend of mine, Peter McGuinness, and I would spend hours watching and listening to John teach at his Blackpool driving range in the winter evenings. I remember there being some very cold sessions watching a clinic or an individual lesson sometimes until 11pm. During these evenings Peter and I would always be invited by John to a complimentary lesson, the knowledge we gained from these experiences for our own golf game, but more importantly for our future coaching skills, was invaluable.

There is no doubt that 'Dr Golf' as John Jacobs became known, has been the world's leading coach. He has the respect of all modern day golf coaches; they give him the credit for raising the standard of coaching technically and also in the way to present the game and oneself.

Over the years coaches and players have been more than willing to share their knowledge and experiences with one another. I remember when Bob Torrance wrote a letter to Ben Hogan stating that he greatly admired him and would it be possible to meet up with him to discuss various aspects of golf and his swing. The meeting took place and Bob gave great credit to Hogan for the technical and other information which he received and used to help his pupils achieve greater success.

Coaches in various sports will ask for advice or help from either their mentor or respected coach. Certainly during my career I have been given sound advice from a number of well-known coaches.

With Bob Harmon & Peter Cowen
The PGA Convention 2003

Training for assistants and the further education programmes for qualified professionals by The PGA are undoubtedly raising the standards of coaching. One convention organised by the PGA in 2003 for further education, was delivered by Butch Harmon and his two brothers Bob and Dick. Other aspects of the game were covered by specialists in their field and the event was a big success.

To be the best coach

- In no particular order or priority you need to:
- Understand the expectations of your pupil.
- Have empathy.
- Be a good listener.
- Have patience.
- Be a motivator.
- Be a giver.
- Have many different ways of communicating.
- Have a thirst for knowledge. You never stop learning.
- Make sure you don't take the thinking away from your pupil.
- Be the eternal optimist.
- Remember there is no substitute for experience, it takes time.
- Have a good attitude, belief and commitment. The ABC of coaching.
- Earn the respect of your pupils.
- Remember that pupils don't care how much you know, until they know how much you care.

What makes a good coach

Respected American football coach John Wooden, who passed away at the age of 99, was possibly the greatest college or professional league coach in history. This man won 10 National Collegiate Athletic Association Tournaments in a row at UCLA, an amazing man, but what was going on inside his mind? John Wooden built other people up to be successful, which in turn made him successful. It is an amazing story. Six of his quotes:

1. Consider the rights of others before your own feelings and the feelings of others before your own rights.
2. A coach is someone who can give correction without causing resentment.
3. Talent is God given, be humble, fame is man given, be grateful, conceit is self-given be careful.
4. You can't live a perfect day without doing something for someone who will never be able to repay you.
5. Do not let what you cannot do interfere with what you can do.
6. Material possessions, winning scores and past reputations are meaningless in the eyes of the Lord because he knows what we really are and that's all that matters.

The secret is in the T-cup

Anyone who has read Sir Clive Woodward's bestselling book "Winning" will immediately recognise the acronym, T-Cup. Every high performing athlete, business leader, serviceman or entrepreneur recognises the value of T-Cup.

PGA Master Professional Tony Bennett
Director of Education for the PGAs of Europe

Israeli guru, Yehuda Shinar, conducted more than 15 years of research into what makes a winner. Shinar has no background in sport but his research work was about trying to identify future business leaders and his views on winners are as follows.

"They are people who deal with challenges based on thinking and not just reacting. There's no secret or wonder behind their success stories. They all share what we call 'winning behaviour' that when analysed, is based on certain rules and principles to which winners are totally committed."

So you may ask where and how is T-Cup applied. The 'Race to Dubai' concludes with the season ending Dubai World Championship where it is possible that a player may face a putt on the final green to win $3,666,660! Sixty players will start the week with the opportunity to win the tournament and so T-Cup will be very important.

I have been fortunate enough to listen to Red Arrows pilot, John Hughes, who clearly stated that their training involved T-Cup. I remember him saying that "to even have a chance to be in the team the pilots have to be at the very top of their profession". In other words, they all know how to fly a plane! So why then do the Red Arrows train every day?

When pilots fly their planes at amazing speeds, in close proximity to each other while completing highly complex acrobatics requiring split second timing, then T-Cup is vital.

The majority of military careers start with a period of physical preparation and yet the key part of the training is to develop 'character' in the recruits. In the heat of the battle all military personnel, and especially those in leadership positions, must demonstrate T-Cup.

T-Cup is the acronym for **"thinking correctly under pressure"** and it is the difference between winning and losing.

Go to any sporting tournament and have the world's number three and four compete against each other and I can assure you that it will be hard to find the differences in the technical, physical and tactical ability of either competitor.

The difference is on how they apply their game when it matters most. Essentially that is what T-Cup is all about.

Apply this when you face a putt to win the beers, beat your own personal best or win the monthly medal.

Suggestions

My definition of skill

Some years ago now I was asked if I could describe skill in three words? My answer was: "creating good habits", not long after this conversation I read an article which went as follows:

Who am I?

"Consider these words carefully: I am your constant companion; I am your greatest helper or your heaviest burden. I will push you on, or drag you down to failure. I am completely at your command, half the things you do you may as well turn over to me and I will do them quickly and correctly, I am easily managed but you must be firm with me. Show me exactly how you would like something done and after a few lessons I'll do it automatically. I am the servant of all great men but of all failures also. Those who are great I have made great, and those who are failures I have made failures. I work with the precision of a scientist and the passion of a patriot. You may use me for profit or use me for ruin; it makes no difference to me. Take me, train me, be firm with me and I will put the World at your feet, but be easy with me and I'll destroy you. Who am I? I am habit.

There is an old Irish proverb that says, a bad habit is like a warm bed, easy to get into but hard to get out of. What are the habits you need to get out of? If you want to know where you will be a year from now check your routine. Change does not happen because of what you know, it happens because of what you do on a daily basis".

Old habits

On arriving at The Open to meet with a player I had been working with for many years I found that his ball control was inconsistent, he had referred to his fault checklist to try and workout which area needed attention but had not found the answer. When I discussed with him and watched him hit some shots, I reminded him about his right hand position on the club, a key point which we had worked on from time to time during the previous eight years. All levels of golfers have times when they slip back into their old habits, it is important to know what they are and know how to correct them. Write them down, call it your "fault check list" even top players need reminding and assuring at times, it's not because they don't know; it's because they have forgotten.

A retired wartime pilot

In 1987 I was giving a lesson to a retired RAF wartime Spitfire / Hurricane pilot. At the end of the lesson he said that what we had been working on during the lesson, (concerning the address position) was exactly what he had to do when flying planes during the war. He called these "vital preparations before take-off". What a good reminder for a pre shot routine "vital preparations before I swing. If a right-handed golfer wants to hit a straight to draw shot and their position at address is pointing left (open), or conversely when a golfer wants to hit a fade shot and is pointing right (closed) then they are working against the basic fundamentals / foundations, which makes it difficult to hit the required shot.

How vital is the position at address?

V.   very
I.   important
T.   to
A.   all
L.   levels of golfers

You can only swing the club as well as the position at address allows. So remember that you should not look for faults in your golf swing before checking for faults at address.

During his playing career Peter Alliss was one of the best ball strikers from tee to green. You only have to look at his record of tournament wins and Ryder Cup appearances to see how good a player he was. Anyone who wins European Opens and tournaments as he did, must also have putted well at some time (it's the name of the game).

Many great players find holing out a struggle at times, especially on distances from 3 to 5 feet, thus leading to loss of confidence. I believe that Peter eventually admitted to not being able to see a line or a way into the hole.

When a golfer is playing well, it's easy, everything seems to fall into place, nothing seems to upset or distract their concentration or flow of the game. So what happens when the opposite happens and everything is a struggle? There can be a number of reasons:

- Thinking about the mechanics of the swing.
- Remembering bad shots and unlucky breaks.
- Loss of confidence and uncertainty in decision making.

Often a player's pre-shot routine changes and they develop a lack of trust in what they have been working on in practice. Being able to visualise the shot starts the process of decision making and everything else follows.

When coaching, the words we use to describe a specific point are so important to the pupil because, words create pictures and pictures create action. This makes the quotation, "As a man thinketh so shall it be", very relevant to the game of golf.

I use and recommend the following model:

1. See it - in the mind
2. Feel it - in the muscles
3. Do it - with a routine

Practice what you preach. See it - feel it - do it and remember that every putt is straight once you have aimed; all you need is the correct speed and pace.

Use your eyes

During the Home International matches which are held once a year, the coaches of the four nations have the opportunity to exchange information and ideas. At the 1994 matches held at Royal Liverpool Golf Club I asked a well-respected friend and coach Bob Torrance, what he thought was required to be a good coach? His immediate answer, "a good eye".

In one of the GUI pre-season youths coaching weeks at La Cala Golf Club in Spain we had panel meetings for an hour each day to discuss various points raised. On the second day course management was on the agenda and many areas were covered, with the overall view from the players being that club selection and the grain on the greens presented difficulties. Good shots with the wrong club make even the calmest individual hot under the collar and constantly having to hole those five or six foot putts eventually leads to three putt greens.

After listening to their remarks and recognising that the courses both had undulating fairways and greens, I suggested that the players use their eyes, to better calculate the slopes. Until then they had tended to concentrate so much on their approach shot and the grain on the greens but had forgotten to estimate the changes in topography. On the third day one of the youths from the panel came to me and showed me a Spanish golf magazine which had just been released that morning. He asked me to look at the article that the great Christy O'Conner Snr had written in which his comments on how to play Valderama Golf Club (where the Ryder Cup was going to be held later that year), made very similar points. Needless to say he thought I must have known about the article, which was not the case, but it is amazing how often we forget the obvious!

The three step process to correct aiming

1. The shot is produced by swinging a club using the joints and muscles of the body.
2. The body receives instruction from the mind.
3. The mind receives its inspiration through the eyes.

Therefore when aiming look attentively not only at the ball but also at the objective point; it may be the hole, direction marker or a specific target point. Harvey Penick always asked his pupils to "take dead aim" so that the eyes will register clearly the thing to be accomplished, after which the mind will instruct the muscles on what has to be done.

Many golfers give a casual glance at the direction of play, or the area, but they do not look attentively at a specific point. The mind must be attentive to a certain point after which it takes time for the eyes to adjust their focus. Once the eyes are focused intently on the objective point the location of that point will be impressively registered on the mind and so ensure that it has all the necessary information to instruct the muscles to control the direction and distance of the required shot.

Your golfing success

The following (in alphabetical order) words apply to most successful people in all sports. The application of these words enables people to be as good as they can be and achieve their ultimate dreams. You may want to add your own words to the list?

- Attitude
- Desire
- Goals
- Memory
- Motivation
- Patience
- Persistence
- Preparation
- Practice
- Self-discipline

How you place these words in order of importance is up to you but for me the number one word is 'desire' after which the others start to make sense.

Padraig Harrington gave a talk to a group of GUI panellists on the 1st December 1996 and described desire as a 'want'. He asked those who would 'like' to play in the Walker Cup and those who would like to turn professional and play in the Ryder Cup to put their hands up and then rephrased the question by changing the word 'like' to the word 'want'. He then stated that only those with a real want would have a chance of success. I am sure you will agree he has proved to be a perfect role model in this regard.

Sir Clive Woodward at the PGA Conference in Coventry 2008 described it as an "obsession" almost to the point of being "obsessed."

Whether you call it want / obsession / or desire, I believe this to be the first priority a player needs to reach his or her potential.

There are no natural born golfers

No person ever entered the world with the natural ability to drive the green on a par 4 or hit a one iron 280 yards. What golfers are born with is desire, desire to work, desire to sweat, desire to learn, desire to have someone watch him / her and say look there we have a natural born golfer.

Preparation is the key to success

On introduction to the players in the various Golfing Union of Ireland panels my motto was "preparation is the key to success" which follows closely from the old adage of 'if we fail to prepare, we prepare to fail".

Today we live in a world of instant, push a button, press a switch, but to improve in anything it requires commitment. Once we remind ourselves of this, understand and accept the principals mentioned, we can start to improve our golf, enjoy the journey and the results will follow.

In order to accomplish our desires the 3D's and the 3P's are required. Successful people in all walks of life apply the following principals in one way or another:

DESIRE   A real want to achieve your dreams.

DISCIPLINE   Controlled behaviour.

DEDICATION   Long term devotion to a purpose.

PATIENCE   Calm endurance of annoyance / hardship.

PERSEVERANCE   Continue steadfastly in spite of difficulties, pursuit of an objective.

PRACTICE   To make permanent, become or remain skilful through correct practice.

Looking at areas of improvements

As you can see from the following self-analysis form, there are many steps to be taken in order to be a complete golfer. We are all different and each golfer will require their own individual programme. It is important to get the basic fundamentals correct and apply common sense and logic. We all have our own golf swings, they are like our fingerprints. All great players have their own individual swings but they all observe the basic fundamentals and apply them.

I feel sure by now you are thinking how and where shall I start this preparation which will improve my golf? You have already made a start by looking for information, you have shown the 'desire or want' which is needed in order to succeed.

Next steps

The next step is to establish your strengths and weakness profile and the best way is to contact a qualified PGA golf professional who will make an assessment and suggest an appropriate programme for you. Alternatively you can use the following self-analysis form. Be very honest when doing your analysis. When completed the sheet indicates those areas which need working on. Once you have established these areas the big question is, what are you going to do about it?

Remember: "Don't neglect your strengths whilst strengthening your weaknesses".

Self-analysis form

Self-Analysis Form					
Name:				Handicap:	
Date:	Address:				
TASK	Poor	Fair	Goo	V	Comments
Tee shots					
Long irons					
Medium irons					
Short irons					
Pitch shots					
Chip & run					
Bunkers					
1/2 -3/4 shots					
Sloping lies					
Putting					
Course strategy					
Mental game					
Attitude					
Preparation					
Fitness					
Greens hit in					
Stroke average					

What to expect when making swing improvements.

If you are making improvements to your swing I am sure that you will realize it takes a little time to re-educate your muscles to do the new movements instinctively, the subconscious mind will also require time to accept the new ideas.

There are three stages the golfer goes through, as a general rule, when making changes.

1. State of confusion
   The conscious mind knows what you are trying to achieve but the subconscious mind still wants to perform in the old way (the ball may go anywhere).

2. Confident on the practice ground
   The new movement is achieved and the ball is under control (but not yet whilst playing on the golf course).

3. Complete confidence on the course
   This is the ultimate, you can trust the new swing, go through your pre shot routine and then go ahead and swing instinctively.

If you find the above is not happening and you are working hard at your game but not getting the results, consider that perhaps you have got to the stage where you should stop working on your game and now it's time to just play, which is an entirely different matter.

The results of working at your game:

- Trying to manufacture the perfect swing (or the perfect swing in your mind) to the point that your score becomes second priority.
- Hitting golf balls until you have lost the ability to swing in reaction to the target.
- Entirely losing the ability to trust your swing once you step on the golf course.
- Becoming addicted to working hard rather than playing your best. Ben Hogan hit more golf balls in practice than most but he would hit around twenty balls then take a rest. At all times Mr Hogan was trying to accomplish one adjustment each time he practiced, once he had accomplished that he would then go on the course and trust it.

Obsession with mechanics

Correct mechanics are important, but over emphasis is futile, there are times when it seems to become an obsession to look text book. Nicklaus, Trevino, Player, Palmer and Furyk found a swing that they could trust, regardless of whether the experts found it visually pleasing or not and each accomplished it on his own or with a teacher and did not care what anyone else thought.

Stop the addiction of working when you should be playing

Separate practice from play as the place to work on your game is on the practice ground, only there should you be concerned with the mechanics of your swing; on the course it's time to trust it. It is very important to educate the mind to think in these two separate ways.

On the practice ground devote 40% of your practice time to mechanics and 60% to playing practice.

Start with work on technique, swing positions etc, this is the time to be a perfectionist. If you are changing your grip make sure you get it correct before every shot, if you are monitoring the first move away from the ball discipline yourself to make this movement just the way you want it to be. Concentrate only on one thing and don't worry if your shots are not flying perfectly.

When you practice, visualise on-course situations and hit shots to imaginary fairways and greens. On all of these shots use your pre shot routine and forget the mechanics. Create a one ball situation, golf is not like tennis where you get two serves, in golf you only get one chance, you have to do it first time.

Preparing for a tournament

Increase the amount of 'play-practice' on the practice ground as the tournament date gets closer, also spend more time on the course and less on the practice ground.

Devote 60% of your practice to the short game

Chipping, putting, pitching and bunker play, remember even if you have perfected your full swing, it would account for only approximately 25% of the average players' score.

Always visualise the shot

Think VAS **V**isualise **A**im **S**wing

Resist the temptation to analyse, if you want to have a swing thought keep it to just one, do not think of mechanics on the golf course, this is the time to trust and it will grow as the round continues.

Learn to score well when playing badly

Learn to tolerate bad breaks and do not make excuses. Learn to win when not at your best and when you can master this skill you will have overcome the mechanics obsession. This means that you are playing and not working at golf.

If you commit yourself to correct practice you will discover that your on course performance can be improved in one or more areas. You must be willing to start with small things and even though when you first start to practice your gains may only be small, they will surely grow. There's a price to pay to reach the next level. Sydney Howard remarked, "One half of knowing is what you must give up before you get it". Too many of us regard practice as an essentially negative experience, but it doesn't have to be if you think of it in terms of discovery and development.

Does practice make perfect?

We often hear or read that practice makes perfect, I believe it is misleading; it encourages us to think that the more we practice the more successful we are going to be. Unfortunately it sometimes has the opposite effect and leads to bad habits, loss of confidence and poor results. The following quotes are what we should be striving for:

- Correct practice makes perfect
- Practice makes permanent
- Quality practice not quantity
- Creating good habits leads to skill and consistency

When it comes to correct practice the most difficult challenges you face are:

- Having the desire to do it.
- Having the discipline to keep at it.
- Having the perseverance and the diligence necessary.
- Being disciplined enough.
- Realising that it has nothing to do with ability.
- Realising that it is not a matter of conditions, but of choice.

Once the choice is made and practice becomes a habit two things become obvious, the first is a clear difference between the person who practices and the one who doesn't. The cyclist Lance Armstrong said success comes from training harder and digging deeper than others and he should know, he won a record seven Tour de France Championships.

The second thing that emerges is a winning spirit. The harder you work, the harder it becomes to surrender to things like fatigue, complacency, discouragement and criticism that can easily break your stride.

Use slopes to change your swing

When making a change to your swing use sloping lies, ball below, ball above, uphill and downhill, this will give you the pictures, feel and swing that you are trying to achieve. If you are going to practice at a driving range find one that has an adjustable mat, this way of practicing will also help you when you are on the golf course, how many times do you get a flat lie?

What are the important contact points, (the foundations)

The Oxford Dictionary describes foundations as "the base, the first layer." There are two contact points in the golf swing, the hands in contact with the club and the feet in contact with the ground, both are the foundations. The grip (hands) is the only connecting point to the golf club. Sir Henry Cotton said "that most golfers miss hit shots due to a grip slip," some great coaches describe the grip as the heart of the golf swing.

The feet are the only connecting point with the ground and they support the upper body. Jack Nicklaus, Bob Torrance, and many more believe good golf starts from the ground upwards.

Provided that these two connecting points are in place and working correctly then building a reliable golf swing can take place.

Practice the one ball drill - the way to avoid three putting

As I have already stated only 'correct' practice makes perfect. Make sure you develop a routine that suits you but I believe this is personal, what suits one does not necessarily suit another, but which ever form of practice session you decide on, I would encourage you to include the 'one ball practice'.

When you go to the putting green and are happy that your stroke and routine are good, then use only one ball to go around the green, this means you will have a new line and a new distance every time which is what happens on

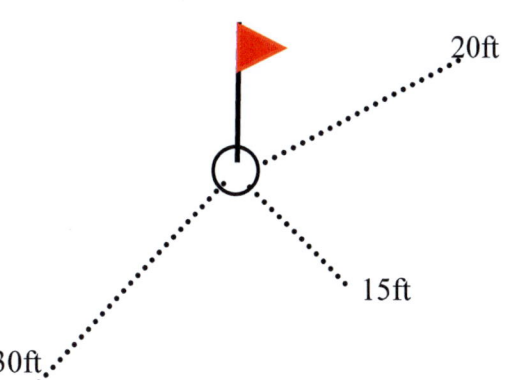

the golf course. Using mental visualisation you can apply one ball practice on the practice range with every club in the bag.

Depending on the time available, here is a suggested practice session:

The biggest single reason for three putting is not judging the correct pace of the first putt. Hand on heart how often do you practice pace putting?

Try this exercise. Take three golf balls onto the practice green; now place each ball a different length from your pre-selected hole.

Your aim is to consistently roll the ball to 9 inches past the hole at the very first attempt from all three distances.

Remember you do not get a second chance on the golf course.

How to lower your scores without changing your swing

Take the following Par 18 short game challenge: Select nine different ball positions around a practice green; see (illustration). Play each ball to the pin and hole out, do not be tempted to play another ball from the original position, we are trying to create the on course situation on a competition day, every shot played in golf has a result, be it good, bad or indifferent, this is why golf is such a challenge. Another difficulty is that as the ball is stationary we have so much time for the mind to think what good or bad things could happen.

You should only take the test once per day. Record your score each day and see if your total score comes down. Your score will reduce with practice and a score of 21-23 would help most players to improve their handicap.

Par 18 short game challenge

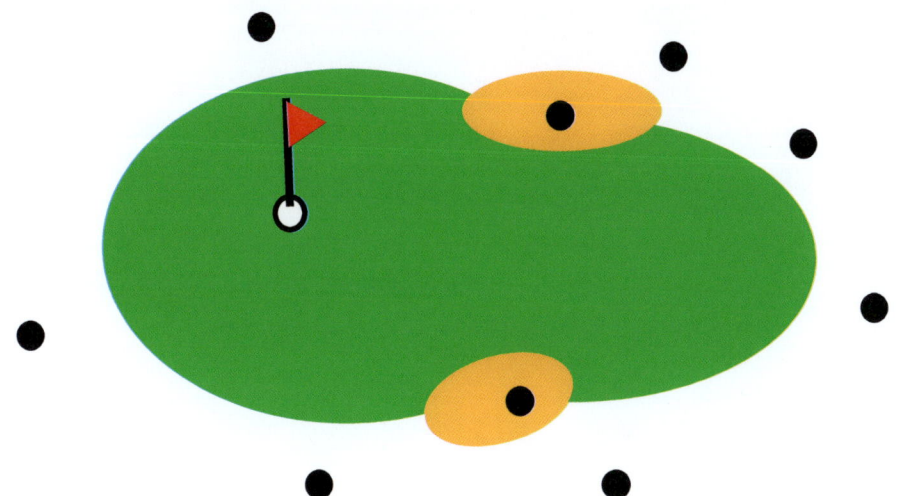

PAR 18 Short Game Challenge (9 holes)

Player:

Marker:

Hole	Score	Comments
1		
2		
3		
4		
5		
6		
7		
8		
9		
Total		

What price success?

1. Nothing in your past guarantees that you will continue growing, with the exception of your commitment to do so.
2. The old Irish proverb says you have to do your own growing, no matter the height of your grandfather.
3. Every new level of growth requires a new level of sacrifice.
4. Can you think of even one person in history who lived an easy life whose name is worth remembering?
5. If you want to grow you will have to deal with loneliness.
6. The majority will always conform, for that is how you get acceptance.
7. The most successful people forge ahead during the time others waste, because they have learned how to be alone.
8. Another price tag for growth is personal responsibility.
9. When are you going to stop using your past as an excuse for living the way you are.
10. Winners focus on what can be, not on what should have been.
11. Coach Bill Russell of the Boston Celtics always told his team, "the game is scheduled we have to play it, so we might as well win, enjoy the challenge."
12. If you want to be a winner you've got to pay the price.
13. I will do today that which others will not, so that I can do tomorrow what others cannot.

Mental reminders

1. You win Major Championships not by playing a continuous series of great shots, but by being prepared for mishaps and setbacks, (it takes a long time to realize this, but I think it is the key). Jack Nicklaus said he rarely played his best golf in the Majors, he won when he was getting up and down from everywhere. Your thinking has to be better than your playing and it's not realistic to expect either to be perfect, strive to get both better than the rest.
2. Be your own best friend, don't berate yourself, would you talk to your best friend that way? Encourage yourself on the course.
3. If you take care of the things you can take care of, the winning will take care of itself.
4. If a player is going to be a great player, he or she must take responsibility for winning.
5. Have you played to the best of your capabilities? Did you enjoy yourself on the course? How did you do against par?
6. To be a match for anyone you must be a good chipper and putter.
7. When making changes in your swing, be patient with yourself, be your own best coach.

Great sayings

1. Don't put yourself down; other people will do this for you.
2. Great people are just ordinary people with an extraordinary amount of determination.
3. Most people fail not because they lack ability, intelligence or opportunity, but because they don't give it all they've got.
4. Faith is daring to risk imperfection.
5. The road to success is always under construction and carries the sign 'work in progress'.
6. Suffering produces perseverance thus leading to character and in turn hope.
7. Prepare for the unexpected.
8. The difference between a 3 handicap and a +3 handicap is: short game, course management and the mind.
9. Your bad shots are not going to go away; it's how you handle them which counts.
10. Does your golf control your attitude or does your attitude control your golf?
11. The will to win is not as important as the will to prepare.
12. Always be the optimist, pessimists always look for excuses.
13. Luck is an acronym for: labouring under correct knowledge.
14. Golf is a simple game, made difficult by human beings

From Kirk Douglas's book – my stroke of luck.

When you feel too weak to carry your burden, look to the actions of other human beings for inspiration. Embedded in my mind is the Seattle Special Olympics of a few years ago. A story was told to me about nine contestants, all physically or mentally disabled, assembled at the starting line for the hundred yard dash.

At the gun, they all started out, not exactly in a dash, but with a relish for running the race to the finish and winning. All that is, except one little boy, who stumbled on the asphalt, tumbled over a couple of times and began to cry.

The other eight heard the boy cry. They slowed down and looked back. Then they all turned around and went back…. Every one of them.

One girl with Down's Syndrome bent down, kissed him and said, "This will make it better". Then all nine linked arms and walked together to the finish line. Everyone in the stadium stood, and the cheering went on for several minutes. People who were there are still telling the story.

Why? Because deep down we know that what matters in this life is more than winning for ourselves. What matters is helping others win, even if it means slowing down and changing our course. We all want happiness. Life teaches us that we achieve happiness when we seek the happiness and well-being of others.

Like Father Like Son

How I came to play golf and made it a career

Like most boys at 11 years of age I was very keen on playing football, swimming and other sports. The year was 1949 and it was when my parents accepted the position of steward and stewardess at Reddish Vale Golf Club near Stockport. Little did I know that it was going to lead to a career in Golf and how much influence the game would have during my life.

Tom Fairbairn was the club Professional at Reddish Vale Golf Club. He was a very good player, and he asked if I would caddy for him and help him in his shop. In return he said that he would give me some lessons and show me how to play the game of Golf. In 1951 my parents moved to become the steward and stewardess at Hillside Golf Club, Southport. This was my first experience of links golf which was a great opportunity.

Two years of national service in the RAF preceded my decision to become the assistant professional at Formby Golf Club near Southport. On completion of my apprenticeship I took up the role of Professional / Green-keeper at Dewsbury and District Golf Club, Mirfield, Yorkshire.

In 1962 I moved to Shaw Hill Golf Club and for the next 15 years was immersed in the life of the traditional Club Professional. A move just down the road to take up the position of Director of Golf at Duxbury Park municipal Golf course followed and for ten years I oversaw the development of the newly opened course. In 1987 I accepted the position of Director of Golf at Penina Golf Course in the Algarve, but my heart was in coaching and so when the position of National Golf Coach to the Golfing Union of

Ireland became available in 1988, I applied and got the job. Looking back it was an honour to be involved in the development of Irish Golf with the GUI, the team of provincial coaches and all the PGA Professionals in Ireland. It was a great privilege to have worked with so many talented young and mature players. I spent 15 years as the National Coach and stayed in the post until my retirement in 2004.

Throughout my life I have been blessed to be involved in so many different areas of golf. During my time as a PGA member the association has undergone many changes. I have been involved as the Chairman of the North Region, a tutor working in the apprentice training programme and as a Director of the Board. In 2000 I was offered and accepted Honorary membership of the PGA and in 2006 I was awarded the distinction of PGA Master Professional.

During my career I have had unconditional support and understanding from my wife, Sylvia, and encouragement from our son, Antony. Thank you both so much.

Words from Tony

My Dad asked for a few words to summarise my career so far. I suppose that it has been quite varied and has evolved over the last 35 years. I never felt pressured into playing golf and only took the game up when a school friend challenged me to a long driving competition. He played for one week, while I am still as passionate about a game of Golf as I was when first starting. School could never compete with Golf. Just as I found school to be boring and less than stimulating, conversely the game held fascination and challenge. On reflection, it is possible to divide my professional career into four distinctly different phases, and who knows, perhaps there will be more.

In any case the first phase could be classed as the initial period, which included PGA training school and the development of whatever talent I might have had for playing the game. Dad was keen for me to complete the PGA training course and I could have had no better mentor. As a trainee I did all the jobs expected of an apprentice, but crucially in a busy club shop. I did have time to practice and play, but suspect that the 6.30am opening shift on Saturday and Sunday morning, which always seemed to be my responsibility, was a way to stop me staying out too late at the weekend! I qualified after three years and became one of the youngest fully qualified professionals in the country. My playing career had a few ups and not many downs, playing anywhere that I could get a start, but overall it could be described as unspectacular, consistent and mildly profitable. Even so I was becoming rich in experience, well-travelled and more clear on the path which the next phase of my career would take.

The second phase of my career started in 1983 when I met my future wife. I had secured my first club professional job at Leyland Golf Club, and had lowered my playing aspirations to competing in regional and national PGA events. A couple of years later with the imminent arrival of our son, we moved across the country to Newark Golf Club, where I applied all the lessons that I had learned, especially those from my first job. We implemented many new ideas and gained a reputation as having a good retail business, but the real success is that I became more engaged in coaching and education with the PGA as a lecturer. This really suited my personality and as a vociferous reader and committed lifelong learner the subject matter was perfect. I was on a very fast learning curve and could develop many of the things that I learned from my Dad both in business and coaching. The next logical step was to build our successful business further and perhaps look for a larger more prestigious club, after all we had been in post for eleven years and I had not been short of offers. This is when the third phase commenced with an opportunity that came out of the blue.

I had been coaching some good young players and had the opportunity to run a training week for the Portuguese National Boys Team during the winter months. The week went well and I was invited back on quite a few occasions. I had a few of the youngsters come to visit our club for coaching and spend a few weeks in the spring. I did what I could to help them develop as players and several of them went on to have national or international success. This prompted an offer of the National Coach position from the Portuguese Golf Federation. I turned down the initial approach and it was only when they came back some months later that I finally accepted.

I thoroughly enjoyed my time working with the Portuguese players and it was a great opportunity to learn from some talented athletes. All coaches learn from the athletes that they work with and when working with good players the quality of their feedback is generally excellent. Often they will ask insightful questions that demand the coach to be at the top of their work. In my last year as National Coach I had started to develop some learning centres and was getting more involved in consultancy work. Perhaps it was the work that I had done with the National team, the learning centres or both, but in 2006 I was very honored to receive the award of, Commendador de Order de Merito, from the President of The Republic of Portugal, for my contribution to sport. On reflection all I really did was keep the focus on helping youngsters to become the best that they could be and instil in them a sense that they should never quit on their dreams and be open to learning.

This brings us to the most recent phase, which is a job in education: quite ironic for someone who could not wait to leave school (although I did successfully complete my 'O' levels)!. My current role is that of Director of Education for The PGAs of Europe, which is an association of associations. We have 38 member countries that in turn have over 18,500 individual professional members. I have been involved with The PGAs of Europe for ten years, first as a member of the Education Committee, then as a Board Director and finally as a member of staff. The role requires me to travel quite a lot and to link the academic world with the practical world in which many professionals reside. I returned to academia (part time) gaining a Master's Degree in Philosophy of Sports Coaching from Birmingham University, which has helped shape my view of the education programmes which we recognise across Europe. I am still a PGA member and was very proud to receive the recognition of PGA Master Professional on the same evening as my Dad. We were presented on the eve of the 2007 Open Championship, which one of Dad's former pupils went on to win. Until today we are the only Father and Son combination to have both received this honour.

So these are my few words. My Dad has been a very positive influence on me: as a person, a golfer, a professional, a learner and an educator. I could have had no better role model.

The 'Friday Club'

Supporting Queenscourt Hospice and North West Cancer Research Fund

On Friday mornings throughout the year a friendly but still competitive match is played by these over 70s. There's plenty of banter and fun at the same time, long may it continue as we still enjoy this wonderful game.

Terry White, member of Formby Hall Golf Club, retired medical representative; played the game all his life.

Tony Coop, PGA professional retired after 45 years of service from Dean Wood Golf Club. Tony qualified for The Open on seven occasions and won the Jersey Open. His best round in tournament play was 61 at Dalmahoy in Scotland. Played in many charity cancer research exhibition matches with Harry Weetman, Max Faulkner & Ken Bousfield.

The author of this book, Howard Bennett

John Donoghue PGA professional retired from Hesketh Golf Club, Southport, after 40 years' service. Practices or plays most days, still plays in the Liverpool Alliance and on many occasions equals or beats his age. John has had 17 holes in one, with his latest being on 3rd March 2011 in the Liverpool Alliance on the 3rd hole at Prenton Golf Club, Cheshire.

Golf poem

In my hand I hold a ball
White and dimpled, rather small
Oh, how bland it does appear
This harmless looking little sphere

By its size I could not guess
The awesome strength it does possess
But since I fell beneath its spell
I've wandered through the fires of hell

My life has not been quite the same
Since I chose to play this stupid game
It rules my mind for hours on end
A fortune it has made me spend

It has made me yell, curse and cry
I hate myself and want to die
It promises a thing called par
If I can hit it straight and far

To master such a tiny ball
Should not be very hard at all
But my desires the ball refuses
and does exactly as it chooses

It hooks and slices, dribbles and dies
and even disappears before my eyes
Often it will have a whim
To hit a tree or take a swim

With miles of grass on which to land
It finds a tiny patch of sand
Then has me offering up my soul
If only it would find the hole

It's made me whimper like a pup
And swear that I will give it up
And take to drink to ease my sorrow
But the ball knows… I'll be back
tomorrow

Supporting cancer research

All proceeds from the sale of this book, less publishing costs, will go to charity.

Thank you for your support.
Howard Bennett.
April 2012

Queenscourt Hospice

Queenscourt

Reg No. 518801

Queenscourt Hospice is an independent charity that provides specialist palliative care to the community in Southport, Formby, West Lancashire and surrounding areas. Opened in 1991 it is largely dependent on voluntary donations to provide the care that all its patients and their relatives deserve. Our services include a ten bedded In Patient unit, a Day Therapy service with many complementary therapies including creative therapy, an Out Patient unit and our new Queenscourt at Home service which recently enjoyed its first birthday. Our Terence Burgess Education Centre runs training courses attended by a wide variety of health professionals and others concerned with caring for the terminally ill. Without the help and support of people who go that little bit extra or that one step further we would not be able to continue providing our exceptional standard of care. We would like to thank everyone who might consider Queenscourt Hospice as the beneficiary of their kindness.

North West Cancer Research Fund

Reg No. 223598

North West Cancer Research Fund
funds pioneering research in the North

West. Were it not for regional cancer research charities like this
new work, potentially the platform on which major breakthroughs
will be made, would never get off the ground. An average of
nearly 90p in every pound raised is spent directly on research.

Printed in Great Britain
by Amazon